THIS JOURNAL BELONGS TO

D1312779

_____

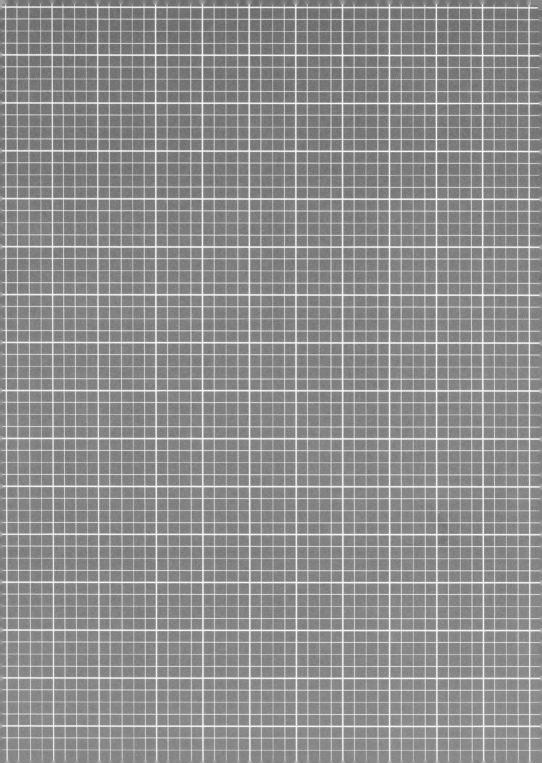

WORK IN PROGRESS

a journal to

SET GOALS • LOG ACCOMPLISHMENTS • TRACK WORK

RENEE BANKS AND TODD PRESLEY

CHRONICLE BOOKS

SAN FRANCISCO

INTRODUCTION

MOST OF US WANT THE SAME THING FROM OUR JOBS: to be challenged by interesting and compelling work, to achieve personal satisfaction through opportunities for growth and learning, and to have colleagues who engage and inspire. Without purpose and direction in our work, the hours can feel long and the days aimless.

The key to finding satisfying work is having a plan. A career plan, like a blueprint, is a step-by-step guide to help you build success at work by setting and achieving small and large goals. It's a record of your journey that can provide insight and inspiration when you most need it. Setting and achieving goals will motivate you to take ownership of your career and instill a passion for achievement and completion that will carry you to the next level in your professional life. It will build satisfaction through self-discovery, which will help as new challenges arise.

This is your space to do just that. Here, you'll reflect on your current work and create a plan with specific goals that you'll track along the way. You'll define what motivates you, catalog your successes and challenges, and take steps to develop your skills and increase your satisfaction. We measure what matters. By taking time to track your progress, you'll get a clearer sense of your accomplishments and professional momentum. You'll also gain perspective, seeing when and where you should shift priorities and direct your efforts into activities that will be more meaningful and rewarding.

HOW TO USE THIS JOURNAL

OVER THE COURSE OF THE NEXT TWELVE MONTHS, your goal is to make progress. Through a series of simple questions and encouraging prompts, this journal will guide you to identify your passion and potential at work and to set achievable and relevant goals. With plenty of space to track your progress against your goals, you'll be able to record meaningful activities, thoughts, and ideas that can be reviewed anytime. Based on what you learn, you'll probably make changes to your approach and the goals themselves over time. Goals that are recorded and checked on regularly are those that have the best chance of being achieved. This journal provides accountability, motivation, and flexibility, and will be your companion along your journey.

You'll start by getting clear on what matters most to you when it comes to your job. Is it your manager who motivates you to do your best work each day? The opportunity to meaningfully impact your workplace? By answering questions about your priorities at work, your career plan will begin to crystallize and you'll be better equipped to define the goals—both short- and long-term—that will help you grow as a professional.

After you've identified your motivations and set goals accordingly, this notebook will guide you month-by-month toward reaching your targets with thought-provoking questions and action-oriented prompts. Each month, you'll be asked to reflect on questions designed to keep you moving forward and building on a set of smaller "mini-goals" that will enable you to achieve the larger ones. This monthly tracking will be a helpful reminder of what you've set out to achieve, which can sometimes get lost in the busy day-to-day shuffle. Spending just a small amount of time each month reflecting on your work will help build momentum that will spur you on.

You don't have to spend a ton of time writing in your notebook each month to benefit from it. The idea isn't to give you extra work on top of your already busy schedule. Writing in this notebook is *you* time, and it's time well-spent. Spending just a quiet half hour a month will help you put your thoughts on paper and perhaps help you see where you can cut down on busywork or unnecessary meetings. These smaller steps and discoveries will lead to breakthrough moments, helping you reach larger goals.

The monthly section will also include space to consider specifically what's worked and what hasn't that month. You'll record:

GOLD STARS

This is a place to take note of all that you've accomplished in a month. Your Gold Stars can be goals achieved, challenges met, or something you did that's unrelated to your core work but nevertheless had an impact. So often, we're working on many projects at once. The victory of completing one can get lost when you're in the midst of executing the rest. Taking a few minutes to record your accomplishments so that you can revisit them can provide inspiration when you need it. Even if it feels like a small win—"I cleaned out my inbox this week!"—here's your space to recognize your successes. You can review these throughout the year (or when it comes time for your annual review) to see how far you've come.

CHALLENGES

Inevitably, roadblocks come up. They are to be expected and, upon examination, relished as unique learning opportunities. In our "fail fast" culture, the bold missteps have much more value than the safe path. Keeping tabs on what, when, and why challenges arise can help redirect your efforts and future planning. Understanding that an unrealistic schedule threw you off course, or that an under-resourced team couldn't deliver, can help you make smarter decisions on the next project or task. Discovering how to adapt to and profit from these challenges will develop your critical thinking skills and propel your career in ways you may not have imagined.

BRIGHT IDEAS

Each month will also feature a Bright Idea. This is a purpose-driven, easily-achieved action you can take that may help you see the bigger picture or expand your horizons. Sometimes we need to step outside of the routine and do something that will help us reach larger goals, or even improve our daily work. For example, going on an informational interview (even if you're not looking for a new job) can broaden your view of your chosen field and introduce you to like-minded people who can share best practices. Bright Ideas provide an impetus to get something done. Once completed, you'll enjoy the satisfaction of doing a little something to help your career, and you can jot down a few notes about the experience. You might even decide to incorporate a little something into your daily, monthly, or annual routine. In the back of this journal, you'll see even more Bright Ideas in case you want a little extra inspiration.

PROGRESS CHECK-INS

When you reach the six-month mark, you'll have the opportunity to check in on the larger goals you defined for yourself at the outset. It's possible that new goals need to be defined, or original goals tweaked. This is natural. Adaptability is important when reviewing and evaluating your goals. Because you'll have half a year's worth of reflection and activity to consider, your path for the next six months should be easy to define.

When you reach the end of the journal, it will be time to look back to see how far you've come. It's likely your goals will have changed and it's certain that you will have learned a great deal about yourself. You will have a wealth of information about important experiences that have shaped the professional you've become. Refer back to these pages at review times, or when you need some inspiration and motivation in your daily work. Armed with this information, you'll be prepared to reflect on your efforts and begin to chart new, even more exciting opportunities in your career.

DEFINING YOUR PURPOSE AND POTENTIAL

THE FIRST STEP IN BECOMING YOUR BEST SELF AT WORK is defining what success means to you. By identifying where you are and where you want to be, you'll be able to determine what goals make sense for you on both a small and large scale. Use this space to think about what makes you happy at work, where you'd like your work to go, and what's been helpful in the past to get you there. The answers you write will help you form goals directly related to what's working and what you want for your future, be it next year or over the next few years.

WHAT'S IT ALL FOR?

PURPOSE IS AT THE HEART OF WHAT YOU DO AND WHY YOU DO IT.
While you may not realize it, purpose is often what gets you out of bed
in the morning—it makes you persevere and try harder. Of course,
each person's purpose is unique. For some, making money is purpose
enough—paying the bills, being able to take a nice vacation, and
generally living well. For others, purpose may be about contributing to
the greater good—helping kids discover new ways of learning, creating
books that inspire scores of people, or literally saving lives in an
operating room. Consider the following questions about purpose and
what motivates and drives you to do your best work every day. You may
not know exactly how your current work fits into your larger purpose
for working, or you may know precisely where you want your work to
be in five or ten years. Either way, thinking about the bigger picture
and how it fits into the day-to-day is always helpful.

- What are you most proud of in your professional life?

- How would you describe the best part of your job to a friend?
  Does this give you a better idea about what energizes you
  about the work you do?

- When is the last time you had a really great day at your job?
  What happened that made it special or unique?

- What made you apply for your current job? Would you pursue
  the same thing today? Why or why not?

- How do you define work/life balance? Do you have it? If not,
  why not?

GOAL SETTING

NOW THAT YOU'RE CLEARER ON WHAT'S IMPORTANT TO YOU AT work, and what's motivating you to be your best, it's time to set goals. Research shows that goal setting is an excellent motivator and, in turn, improves performance. Precise goals help us see improvement (or not) and let us identify areas where we need to course-correct. Even minor improvements can lead to big changes over time. One popular goal setting method is to take the SMART approach (SMART = Specific, Measurable, Achievable, Realistic, Timebound). This means setting goals that are clear, can be calculated, are realistic, and have a deadline. Variations exist, but this is a generally accepted model that helps put your desired outcomes in a useful framework. It will help you break down your large goals into manageable chunks to enable small wins over time. SMART goals are easy to check in with and that helps with accountability. Here's how it breaks down, with examples:

	ORIGINAL GOAL	SMART GOAL
SPECIFIC	Improve my professional network.	Join one professional organization and attend one networking event every six months.
MEASURABLE	Sell more advertising space.	Meet or exceed advertising targets by 10% each month.
ACHIEVABLE	Empty my inbox every night.	End the day with the same number of emails or fewer than I started with.
REALISTIC	Never be late to work again.	Set my alarm for thirty minutes earlier each day and plan to be at my desk thirty minutes before my first meeting.
TIMEBOUND	Revisit my career journal often.	Revisit my career journal on the 15th and 30th of each month. Set a calendar reminder on my computer or phone to keep me in check.

SETTING ANNUAL GOALS

Throughout the year, you'll be focusing on goals to help you track your development. Many of these will be small and easily achieved, but some large goals take time, patience, and might always be a work in progress. Consider your answers to the "What's It All For" section and think about what three goals will help you be a more efficient, satisfied, and productive worker this year. Ask yourself: What will define success for me this year? What's the next realistic role in my career path? What needs to happen to get there? These will be the larger goals you'll focus on this year, though they may shift or change as the months go by. Think of them as a starting point for tracking your progress and reminding yourself of what's important this year, but give yourself room to revise these goals as circumstances change. Record these goals on the following pages (and be sure to use the SMART framework). Use the To Consider questions to help you create a mini-action plan for getting started. You may also want to post your goals on a bulletin board or somewhere you can see them while you work. They'll remind you of your purpose and motivation.

goal one: Study for longer. 30 minutes at least a day. Make a resource of study once a week e.g. flashcards.

TO CONSIDER:

▶ How is this goal relevant to your current work?

It will help me achieve good marks in the exams.

▶ How will you achieve this goal? Write down the main steps you (and others) need to take to reach the goal.

Go to the library, clear and organise room, be motivated

▶ What resources, support, and time do you need?

Library, textbooks, internet access.

▶ How does this goal relate to your longer-term career aspirations?

It will give me a wider choice for choosing a career

▶ How will you know if you're successful? Outline the criteria you will use to measure your progress.

My test and exam marks. Also, how I feel

goal two: Become more organised with my room and school work. Make life easier.

TO CONSIDER:

▶ How is this goal relevant to your current work?

It will help me become more calm and make things easier

▶ How will you achieve this goal? Write down the main steps you (and others) need to take to reach the goal.

Tell myself that I'll feel better once I clean/organise my stuff!

▶ What resources, support, and time do you need?

20 minutes each night if not too busy, folders, notebooks, space for items

▶ How does this goal relate to your longer-term career aspirations?

It will make me more calm towards things and I'll be organised from habit.

▶ How will you know if you're successful? Outline the criteria you will use to measure your progress.

I'll be organising and tidying without knowing

goal three: _Look into subjects more and read through/into them deeper._

TO CONSIDER:

▶ How is this goal relevant to your current work?

I will understand things more easily

▶ How will you achieve this goal? Write down the main steps you (and others) need to take to reach the goal.

Go on the internet and read into the subject greater

▶ What resources, support, and time do you need?

Internet, textbooks. books. 30mins - 2hours a week

▶ How does this goal relate to your longer-term career aspirations?

I will find things more interesting and find subjects more easy to follow

▶ How will you know if you're successful? Outline the criteria you will use to measure your progress.

I will find myself looking into things more deeply.

CONGRATULATIONS! You've defined what you want to achieve over the next twelve months by examining your purpose and motivations, and approaching your goals in a SMART way. Now it's time to start tracking those goals.

MONTHLY
CHECK-INS

MONTH
1

{ DATE } _____

CHECK YOURSELF

▶ What's the most exciting thing you did at work in the last few weeks?

▶ What's one thing you want to get done in the next thirty days?
What's stopping you?

▶ If you could change one thing about your job, what would it be and why?
What can you do to change it?

GOALS CHECK

Refer back to your annual goals. What progress have you made on these goals? Do any of them need revising? Make note of tweaks you'd like to make, or if you've dropped a goal completely and wish to add a new one.

goal 1:

goal 2:

_____

_____

_____

_____

_____

_____

goal 3:

_____

_____

_____

_____

_____

_____

_____

GOLD STARS

Record your biggest wins.
Take note of any details that will help you succeed in the future.

▶

CHALLENGES

Jot down some situations that didn't go quite as planned or moments of frustration. What will you do differently next time?

_____

_____

_____

_____

_____

_____

_____

_____

_____

_____

_____

_____

_____

_____

_____

_____

bright idea

Think about the last time you felt empowered at work. What happened? Is it repeatable?

MONTH
2

{ DATE } _____

CHECK YOURSELF

▶ What's the most exciting thing you did at work in the last few weeks?

▶ What's one thing you want to get done in the next thirty days?
What's stopping you?

▶ If you could change one thing about your job, what would it be and why?
What can you do to change it?

GOALS CHECK

Refer back to your annual goals. What progress have you made on these goals? Do any of them need revising? Make note of tweaks you'd like to make, or if you've dropped a goal completely and wish to add a new one.

goal 1:

goal 2:

goal 3:

GOLD STARS

Record your biggest wins.
Take note of any details that will help you succeed in the future.

▶

CHALLENGES

Jot down some situations that didn't go quite as planned or moments of frustration. What will you do differently next time?

bright idea

Attend a networking event. Make a point to talk to at least two new people. (If you have business cards, bring them along!)

MONTH
3

{ DATE } _____

CHECK YOURSELF

▶ What's the most exciting thing you did at work in the last few weeks?

▶ What's one thing you want to get done in the next thirty days? What's stopping you?

▶ If you could change one thing about your job, what would it be and why? What can you do to change it?

GOALS CHECK

Refer back to your annual goals. What progress have you made on
these goals? Do any of them need revising? Make note of tweaks you'd
like to make, or if you've dropped a goal completely and wish to add
a new one.

goal 1:

goal 2:

....

....

....

....

....

....

goal 3:

....

....

....

....

....

....

....

GOLD STARS

Record your biggest wins.
Take note of any details that will help you succeed in the future.

▶ ....
....
....
....

▶ ....
....
....
....

▶ ....
....
....
....

CHALLENGES

Jot down some situations that didn't go quite as planned or moments of frustration. What will you do differently next time?

------

bright idea

Finish a task you've been avoiding. Often checking just one thing off the to-do list can make you feel more productive.

MONTH
4

{ DATE } _____

CHECK YOURSELF

▶ What's the most exciting thing you did at work in the last few weeks?

▶ What's one thing you want to get done in the next thirty days?
What's stopping you?

▶ If you could change one thing about your job, what would it be and why?
What can you do to change it?

GOALS CHECK

Refer back to your annual goals. What progress have you made on
these goals? Do any of them need revising? Make note of tweaks you'd
like to make, or if you've dropped a goal completely and wish to add
a new one.

goal 1:

goal 2:

....

....

....

....

....

....

....

....

goal 3:

....

....

....

....

....

....

....

....

....

GOLD STARS

Record your biggest wins.
Take note of any details that will help you succeed in the future.

▶ ....

....

....

....

▶ ....

....

....

....

▶ ....

....

....

....

CHALLENGES

Jot down some situations that didn't go quite as planned or moments of frustration. What will you do differently next time?

bright idea

Clean out your inbox (or resolve to get it to a certain number of emails by Friday afternoon). Seeing the bottom of your inbox can be exhilarating!

MONTH
5

{ DATE } _____

CHECK YOURSELF

▶ What's the most exciting thing you did at work in the last few weeks?

▶ What's one thing you want to get done in the next thirty days?
What's stopping you?

▶ If you could change one thing about your job, what would it be and why?
What can you do to change it?

GOALS CHECK

Refer back to your annual goals. What progress have you made on these goals? Do any of them need revising? Make note of tweaks you'd like to make, or if you've dropped a goal completely and wish to add a new one.

goal 1:

goal 2:

goal 3:

GOLD STARS

Record your biggest wins.
Take note of any details that will help you succeed in the future.

▶

CHALLENGES

Jot down some situations that didn't go quite as planned or moments of
frustration. What will you do differently next time?

bright idea

Imagine yourself in ten years.
What credentials do you have
and what got you there?

6-MONTH CHECK-IN

CONGRATULATIONS FOR STAYING ON TRACK! This is the perfect time to check on the goals you set and on the progress you've made. Look back over your monthly entries to identify themes across your Gold Stars and Challenges. And what about those Bright Ideas—what have you learned?

{ DATE } _____

GOALS CHECK-IN

What successes have you had for each of your original goals?

goal 1:

goal 2:

goal 3:

What didn't work in achieving your goals? What parts of your plan need retooling to help you achieve the rest of your goals?

goal 1:

goal 2:

goal 3:

Which goals still need attention? Which need to change as a result
of changing priorities at work? Write a mini-plan for each goal you set
(refer back to the To Consider questions in the Annual Goals section
for help).

goal 1:

goal 2:

goal 3:

PROGRESS CHECK: **GOLD STARS**

What's going well that you can build on or repeat?
What positive feedback have you received this year?

▶

CHALLENGES

What obstacles have you been able to overcome? What still needs
to change and what will you do differently to address it over the next
six months? What tools or resources do you need to avoid similar
challenges over the next six months?

MONTH 7

CHECK YOURSELF

▶ What's the most exciting thing you did at work in the last few weeks?

▶ What's one thing you want to get done in the next thirty days?
What's stopping you?

▶ If you could change one thing about your job, what would it be and why?
What can you do to change it?

GOALS CHECK

Refer back to your annual goals. What progress have you made on these goals? Do any of them need revising? Make note of tweaks you'd like to make, or if you've dropped a goal completely and wish to add a new one.

goal 1:

goal 2:

goal 3:

GOLD STARS

Record your biggest wins.
Take note of any details that will help you succeed in the future.

▶

CHALLENGES

Jot down some situations that didn't go quite as planned or moments of frustration. What will you do differently next time?

bright idea

Sign up for a class at your local community college that will help your professional development. Start a discussion group (in person or online) with a couple of classmates.

MONTH
8

{ DATE } _____

CHECK YOURSELF

▶ What's the most exciting thing you did at work in the last few weeks?

▶ What's one thing you want to get done in the next thirty days?
What's stopping you?

▶ If you could change one thing about your job, what would it be and why?
What can you do to change it?

GOALS CHECK

Refer back to your annual goals. What progress have you made on these goals? Do any of them need revising? Make note of tweaks you'd like to make, or if you've dropped a goal completely and wish to add a new one.

goal 1:

goal 2:

goal 3:

GOLD STARS

Record your biggest wins.
Take note of any details that will help you succeed in the future.

▶
▶
▶

CHALLENGES

Jot down some situations that didn't go quite as planned or moments of frustration. What will you do differently next time?

bright idea

Ask someone close to you what your blind spots are. For one week this month, pay particular attention to improving in those areas.

MONTH
9

CHECK YOURSELF

▶ What's the most exciting thing you did at work in the last few weeks?

▶ What's one thing you want to get done in the next thirty days?
What's stopping you?

▶ If you could change one thing about your job, what would it be and why?
What can you do to change it?

GOALS CHECK

Refer back to your annual goals. What progress have you made on these goals? Do any of them need revising? Make note of tweaks you'd like to make, or if you've dropped a goal completely and wish to add a new one.

goal 1:

goal 2:

_____

_____

_____

_____

_____

_____

goal 3:

_____

_____

_____

_____

_____

_____

GOLD STARS

Record your biggest wins.
Take note of any details that will help you succeed in the future.

▶

CHALLENGES

Jot down some situations that didn't go quite as planned or moments of frustration. What will you do differently next time?

bright idea

Ask a peer or your boss for some feedback if you didn't receive any this month. Ask them to be specific about how your actions impact your work.

MONTH
10

{ DATE } _____

CHECK YOURSELF

▶ What's the most exciting thing you did at work in the last few weeks?

▶ What's one thing you want to get done in the next thirty days?
What's stopping you?

▶ If you could change one thing about your job, what would it be and why?
What can you do to change it?

GOALS CHECK

Refer back to your annual goals. What progress have you made on these goals? Do any of them need revising? Make note of tweaks you'd like to make, or if you've dropped a goal completely and wish to add a new one.

goal 1:

goal 2:

_____

_____

_____

_____

_____

_____

_____

goal 3:

_____

_____

_____

_____

_____

_____

_____

_____

GOLD STARS

Record your biggest wins.
Take note of any details that will help you succeed in the future.

▶

CHALLENGES

Jot down some situations that didn't go quite as planned or moments of frustration. What will you do differently next time?

bright idea

Find a mentor. This could be someone inside your company or outside it. Set up a regular meeting schedule, even if it's every six months.

NOTES

MONTH
11

{ DATE } _____

CHECK YOURSELF

▶ What's the most exciting thing you did at work in the last few weeks?

▶ What's one thing you want to get done in the next thirty days?
What's stopping you?

▶ If you could change one thing about your job, what would it be and why?
What can you do to change it?

GOALS CHECK

Refer back to your annual goals. What progress have you made on these goals? Do any of them need revising? Make note of tweaks you'd like to make, or if you've dropped a goal completely and wish to add a new one.

goal 1:

goal 2:

....

....

....

....

....

....

....

goal 3:

....

....

....

....

....

....

....

GOLD STARS

Record your biggest wins.
Take note of any details that will help you succeed in the future.

▶ ....

....

....

....

▶ ....

....

....

....

▶ ....

....

....

....

CHALLENGES

Jot down some situations that didn't go quite as planned or moments of frustration. What will you do differently next time?

bright idea

Invite a respected colleague to coffee. Come prepared with a few questions that will help you learn about that person's career journey.

MONTH
12

{ DATE } _____

CHECK YOURSELF

▶ What's the most exciting thing you did at work in the last few weeks?

▶ What's one thing you want to get done in the next thirty days?
What's stopping you?

▶ If you could change one thing about your job, what would it be and why?
What can you do to change it?

GOALS CHECK

Refer back to your annual goals. What progress have you made on these goals? Do any of them need revising? Make note of tweaks you'd like to make, or if you've dropped a goal completely and wish to add a new one.

goal 1:

goal 2:

_____

_____

_____

_____

_____

_____

_____

goal 3:

_____

_____

_____

_____

_____

_____

_____

_____

GOLD STARS

Record your biggest wins.
Take note of any details that will help you succeed in the future.

▶

CHALLENGES

Jot down some situations that didn't go quite as planned or moments of frustration. What will you do differently next time?

bright idea

Make a list of websites relevant to your field. Use an RSS reader to keep track of important developments.

REFLECTION

OVER THE PAST TWELVE MONTHS, you've taken the time to record and track your goals. The mere fact that you've given yourself the time to pause and reflect on your work is an accomplishment in and of itself. With a year's worth of information at your fingertips, you're now able to go back and look at the patterns that emerged on a daily, weekly, and monthly basis. This is a record of your eureka moments, your problem-solving process, and your triumphs. Look back at how you defined your purpose one year ago. Do those reasons still hold true? Has writing in this notebook shaped those reasons or changed them? If you need to get ready for an annual review, everything you need is right here. Even if you don't have a review to write, think about what you have learned about the way you work and what is next for you.

Looking back over the past year, what are the three accomplishments that make you most proud?

1. ....

2. ....

3. ....

What did you learn from these accomplishments and why do they make you proud?

What were your three biggest challenges over the past year?

1.

2.

3.

What did they teach you and how will you avoid them in the future?

What are three new goals you want to set for yourself?

1.

2.

3.

HAVE YOU NOTICED how your tracking this past year has informed your plans for the future? You've spent the last year practicing and honing your career development skills. You've set goals, reviewed your progress, and identified the patterns of behavior that matter. From here on, you can stand back and see what needs to change and figure out how to make those changes happen, step by well-planned step. All you need to do now is turn the page and keep working.

EVEN
MORE
BRIGHT
IDEAS

- Offer to take a task off a coworker's plate. Choose a task that will expose you to something new or help you develop a skill.

- Go on a mock interview for a job in your field that you don't intend to take. The preparation and practice will inspire you to think about your own career and how to get to the next level.

- Find a subject at work that no one else understands. Write up a plan to learn about it and become the go-to expert.

- Start a monthly "lunch and learn" series with your colleagues. Have people share information about their work and their careers so people can learn from one another.

- Start using a daily to-do list. For one week, take five minutes each morning when you first get to work to organize your day. Review your progress at the end of the week.

- Volunteer to sit on a career panel at your alma mater. Share your work experiences with students and get the benefit of learning by teaching.

- Ask a respected colleague for a book recommendation and then read it. Follow up to discuss the book (and strengthen your relationship).

- Research someone you admire professionally. Jot down a few qualities that you'd like to develop in your own work style.

- Determine one resource that's available to you that you're not using. Make an effort to take advantage of it this month.

- Take a best practice from another company and incorporate it into your work.

- Delegate or collaborate on a task you would normally do by yourself.

- Pick the brain of someone from another generation. What can they teach you about improving your work?

- Update your professional online profile. Don't have one? Create it!

- Research professional organizations in your area and attend a meeting, workshop, or event. Exchange contact information with a new acquaintance.

- Give positive feedback to a deserving coworker. People love to know that someone else is paying attention.

- Do something that makes you uncomfortable at work, but that will ultimately make you better.

- Write a personal value statement. In two or three sentences, describe your current role and forecast the future value of your work to the organization.

- Make a five-minute presentation at work about something you learned this month.

- Join an online professional group. Post one question or observation this month.

- Update your resume. Even if you're not actively searching for a new job, this exercise can help you think about where you've been and what you are doing now.

- Pick up the current issue of a business magazine that you don't typically read. Consider how the contents make you think about your own work.

- If you work for a public company, read the annual report. If not, read the annual report of a company you admire.

- Read your organization's mission statement. Ask yourself how you contribute to that mission.

- Find a respected column or blog in your field and follow it. Share an article or anecdote with your team this month along with your thoughts.

- Write five thank-you notes to colleagues. Be specific about what they did for you or your team, what the context was, and how it positively impacted you.

- Volunteer your time with an organization that can benefit from your expertise and experience. Giving is its own reward, but you'll also benefit from a new opportunity to practice your profession.